Vivien Romhoffer

Macrame for Beginners
– Super Easy Instructions

Table of Contents

Introduction

Macrame, a word whose sound alone is telling you that there is a wonderful kind of magic behind it. Alternatively, you could describe it as tying together threads and tightening them with knots.

As a matter of fact, that's exactly what we're doing every day, however without given it a think. Tying one thread to another, you produce a simple knot. And tying several knots in a row, you're getting a full hank. From a greater quantity of knots, you can easily create entire mats and carpets. Numerous patterns are possible, depending on which kind of knots and which threads are used in the process.

And though so many great patterns can be made, you need nothing else than threads in order to create wonderful and singular works of art. Whosoever thinks that special and expensive tools were needed, is wrong. Nothing like that is necessary. People around the globe know Macrame and love it. And it's likely appreciated for its easy handling.

In Macrame works of art you may find many herbal or animal patterns which is an indication for the use of traditional elements from different cultures. By making these simple knots you are able to create trendy accessories, pieces of decoration, buttons, listellos and many items more.

In this book you will also have the chance to explore the diversity of the art of knotting for your personal use. Be cordially invited to re-create and try out for yourself all those patterns depicted and explained in this book.

Advice: Before you start working with Macrame, you should read through the theoretical part of this book, in which you will be given much insight about it and therefore be granted much easier access to the different weaving and knotting techniques. Anyway, I wish you a great success!

Chapter 1
What is Macrame?

Instantly, there is an image before your eyes when hearing the word Macrame? Perhaps the term "Macrame" might sound familiar to you, but you can't really place it? If yes, this is the right place to be! I'm going to explain to you what Macrame is and where it originally came from. If you have read through the theory of Macrame, it will be easier for you to continue with the practical part of this book, and, finally, put things you learned into practice.

Macrame: This is the way the word is written in Spanish which, however, wouldn't let you know which kind of art the word is concealing. The main focus of Macrame is placed on knots. Knots, you might wonder now. But yes, it's about knots, or to be more accurate, about very artful knots.

Macrame is a weaving technique whose origins are to be found in the Near East. It is used to produce textiles, jewellery and ornaments. The Spanish term "Macramé" is known to Arabic as "Migramah". In the whole Arabic-speaking world this word is taken to denote "weaving". But what has it got to do with the process of tying? Very easy: There is another word, namely "Miqrama", which means translated something like "tied veil".

The pieces of art which can be created by means of the Macrame knotting technique are genuine and unique works done by hand. None is like the other. And it's wonderful to see that these artful pieces can have different sizes. Some do have a length of a few centimetres, while others can be up to ten meters long.

If you consider the wider meaning of the word "Macrame", you could say that it denotes the art of tying threads by means of knots and thus create decorative master-pieces. You can make use of every ribbon, string, every thread and every cord, if usable for tying knots. Usually, people take threads made of hemp, jute, cotton or even silk. Knitting yarn, knitting wool, synthetic threads or even so-called "kite line" are also suitable in a wonderful way. Now, if you wish to try out tying for yourself, you may use every kind of thread you find in your house.

Traditionally, Macrame is used in different ways, even for creating border ornaments like for scarves or tablecloths. Classical elements of decoration include Macrame tassels. If you become accustomed to this technique step-by-step, you will soon realize that you know more about it than you might have thought.

Chapter 2
History

Whosoever tries to ascertain the historical origins of Macrame, will find many different theories because its origins can't be precisely determined. Presumably, this technique was developed in times when man was to use a tool for the first time ever.

In Japan, for example, there were several settlements during the Jomon-period (approx. 14,000 to 300 BC), one of which is Sannai-Maruyama, located southwest of the city of Aomori. Archaeologists unearthed a vine and wristband in a tomb, which argues the existence of this tying technique in these very early times. The name "Jomon" denotes a rope pattern which was pressed onto ceramic jars.

Several researchers take the view that those rope patterns express the religious beliefs of the people. The knots are supposed to be imbued with magical powers and to further the fertility of women. Moreover, the knots are regarded as lucky charms or protective symbols.

But the Macrame tradition can't only be traced back to ancient Japan. This technique is easy to use and can be found scattered all over the world. It was cultivated in most different traditions and cherished by many cultures and exists until the present day.

Children, for example, are taught how to tie ribbons and bows, something which is part of their daily life. This makes knotting a common knowledge passed on to every new generation. You can almost say that Macrame is like a thread running through all our lives.

So, you see, it appears improbable to determine the exact origins of this tying technique. The same applies to the question of how Macrame has made its way to present-day decorative design. The various techniques of knotting became more and more refined in the course of time.

It's possible to proceed from the assumption that the Macrame technique evolved in Western Asia, Eastern Europe, the Near East, as well as Northern Africa. When casting a look back into medieval times, you will be quick to see that the Macrame technique was brought from the Islamic world into Italy and Spain by traders. But the technique was also developed in European countries outside the world of trade. Italian artisans, for example, may have created the greatest variety of knotting techniques.

There are ladies' dresses from the 16th and 17th century which reveal early decorative features. You can see typical knot works embellishing the borders of skirts and dresses.

It was in the 19th century when the queen would teach these techniques to the ladies-in-waiting. Macrame gained great popularity there. The soft ornaments were made of purest silk.

In colonial times these techniques were spread all over the world. It came to Mexico with the Spanish, with the French to Canada (particularly to Quebec) and from Genoa to the Americas.

As mentioned above, the word "Macrame" became an Arabic loan-word in the French language. Later, it was translated into English. People all over the world understand what it means.

Chapter 3
Macrame Today

Not only is this beautiful knotting technique known all over the world, it is also widely appreciated until the present day. As mentioned elsewhere, Macrame is literally running like a thread to all our lives.

It's in popular use when it comes to items of decorative purpose and handicraft. However, all these wonderful accessories are rarely self-made today. There is hardly anyone anymore dedicating time and enthusiasm to such a project of art for a longer period of time.

The heyday of Macrame is over and was in the Seventies and Eighties of the last century. You could find Macrame works in almost every home at those days. Many people, especially women, made Macrame their hobby. But then, slowly, people lost more and more interest in this art. And the only remainder of it you could find were simple trends like braiding or the knotting of scooby doo ribbons.

But that's how things go, but people's interest in such hobbies appear to get stronger again, or you wouldn't have got yourself this book.

Chapter 4
First Steps into the World of Macrame

Before you start off with your first knotting projects, you should make yourself acquainted with the most important basics. Without these basics, you will become desperate fairly soon, and your project might become either bothersome or turn out to be a failure in the end.

These basics include that you know about the range of knots you can make. Here we go:

The Overhand Knot

Take the cord, make a wrap, and bring the top end through the loop. Then pull both ends to tighten the knot.

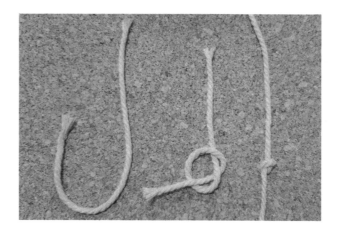

The Wave Knot

You need a total of two cords, preferably in different colours. I, for example,
choose the colours yellow and red.
Take the red cord and bring it over and
under the yellow cord. Then, criss-
cross both cords so that you obtain two
loops. After that, bring the end of each
cord through the loops. Both ends can
now be tightened.

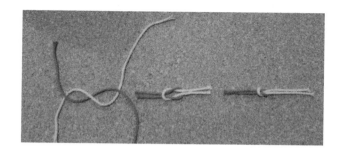

The Loop Knot

You need a total of four cords. Place
three of them next to each other on the
table. Then take one of them as working cord and bring it under the other
three cords, move it over them and
then through the produced loop. Finally, tighten the ends of the working cord.

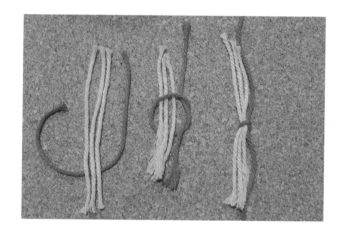

The Fisherman's Knot

Move the lower end of the cord over its upper end, thus producing a loop. Then take the end of the cord and make three wraps around the left side of the loop. Hold fast its lower end and pull the upper end protruding through the loop out of it.

The Wrap Knot

You need several cords. First, double the working cord. Then wrap its lower end around the filler cord as often as possible and feed the wrapping cord into a loop. Then, pull the upper end of the wrapping cord upwards so that the knot disappears under the wrapping. Finally, cut off both wrapping ends.

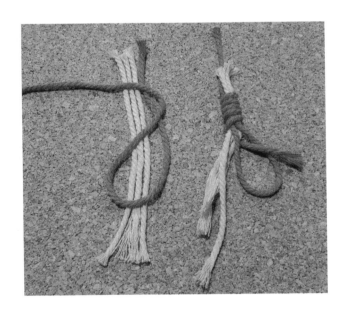

The Figure Eight Knot

Place a cord on the table. Pass its lower end over itself to form the figure eight. Continue over and under the cord, so it can be passed through the lower belly of the eight. Then tighten the knot at both ends.

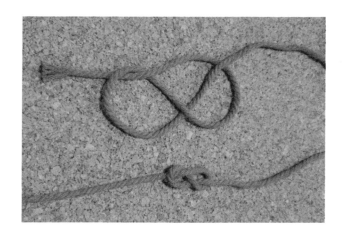

The Cable Trek

Place two cords next to each other, preferably in two different colours. With its lower end bring the right cord to the left over and then under the second cord. The left cord is then placed under and over the right cord. Feed it into the loop which was first produced. With one hand you hold the knot fast, while with your other hand you tighten first the left and then the right cord.

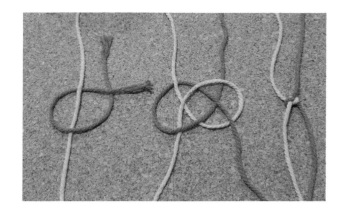

The Carrick Bend / The Reef Knot

Place four cords next to each other. Take the outermost cord on the left and place it over the other cords in such a manner as to form an L. Then move the outermost cord on the right over the L-shaped cord, under the middle cords and, finally, through the loop. Repeat everything the other way round. The right reef knot is knotted the same way; however, you start off on the right side.

The Anchor Knot

Place the working cord over and under the middle cords. Then feed the working cord into the loop and tighten the knot. Repeat everything and tighten the knot.

Right Anchor Knot:

Left Anchor Knot:

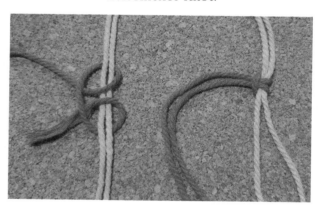

Clove Hitch

Make sure that the working cord is longer than the other cords. Place the working cord over the other cords in such as manner as to form an L. This cord is never pulled tight, but only hold fast. Now, take the first cord next to the working cord and move it under and over the working cord and, finally, through the loop. This procedure is always repeated to make sure the knot is tight enough. To make the Left Clove Hitch you start off on the left side, the Right Clove Hitch on the right side.

Right Clove Hitch:

Left Clove Hitch:

The Round Chinese Knot

You need a total of four cords. Place the first cord over the second cord to produce a loop. The second cord is then placed over the third cord and the third placed over the fourth. You've got three loops now. Then pass the fourth cord through the first loop and pull the cords tight.

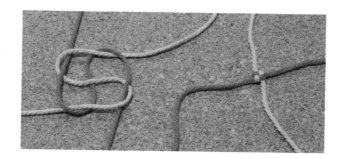

Chapter 5
Materials

Whosoever wishes to try out the Macrame technique should know which materials are needed for which purpose, I compiled a list for you. It's supposed to be a means of orientation. However, you should also be aware of the fact that for every project specific materials are required, which are never the same.

- ❖ Threads made of: Cotton, Jute, Hemp, synthetic materials
- ❖ Sewing thread
- ❖ Twigs from the wood
- ❖ Driftwood: From rivers or lakes
- ❖ Wooden sticks (DIY store)
- ❖ Wooden balls
- ❖ Wooden letters
- ❖ Wooden rings
- ❖ Glasses (especially for lanterns)
- ❖ Metal rods
- ❖ Metal rings
- ❖ Key rings
- ❖ Scissors
- ❖ Tape measure
- ❖ Comb
- ❖ Crotchet hooks in different sizes
- ❖ Notepad (for planning projects)
- ❖ Gloves (good for stronger threads)
- ❖ Bulletin board
- ❖ Pins
- ❖ Duct tape
- ❖ Pad
- ❖ Different pendants

In order to make sure your first ever Macrame projects will be successful, I would like to enter into a detailed description of some of the materials in the following part. These materials, by the way, are most widely used for all the fantastic knot-projects of Macrame.

Cotton Threads

These threads are perfect for knotting friendship wristbands or lanyards. You can get it in different colours. Cotton yarn is known for its extraordinary power of resistance, which guarantees you long durability of everything you may knot. Particularly in summer when it's hot outside, you prefer going into the cool water. Wouldn't it be bothersome, if you had to take off your friendship wristbands all the time? If you knot them with cotton threads, there's no problem wearing them in water. Water can't do any damage to it. The cotton just gets wet, just like yourself. In the industrial production of cotton yarn certain other components are added which prevent the hardening of the threads.

Among the many upsides of cotton threads there is also one downside I should mention: Cotton yarn has got an incredible suction power, for which reason it will take some time for your friendship wristband to become dry again.

Cotton yarn isn't only available in various colours; you can also make your choice between two variants: There is twisted cotton yarn or braided cotton yarn. If you plan a knotting project that requires the ends of the threads to be combed out, you best go for twisted cotton yarn. It can be combed out much easier. Another point to be considered is that twisted cotton yarn is less expensive.

Apart from that, cotton wool ropes are highly appreciated for knotting projects and widely in use. Cotton wool ropes are particularly used for bigger knotting projects like table runners or even tablecloths, since it's stronger than regular cotton yarn. Despite being very soft, it's got good stability. If you wish to get yourself a cotton wool rope, please bear in mind that its elasticity is diminished with the thickness of the rope itself.

Silk

Silk is very skin-friendly, for which reason it's very suitable for Macrame projects. Especially for people suffering from allergy, silk is a wonderful alternative to other materials. Because of its breathing activity, wet silk can dry very quickly. However, it's important to know that you have to hand-wash Macrame objects made of silk, since the cleaning in your washing machine would be too strong and cause damage to the soft material.

Linen

This material is likewise very suitable for knotting great things. It's very easy-care and also tear-proof. Its skin-compatibility is very high, too, for which reason you can easily use it for making friendship wristbands.

Wool

In order to create Macrame pieces of art, wool is by far the cheapest variant to go for. Its properties include elasticity and breathability. It's also important to know that there are species of wool that can be scratchy on our skin. If you wish to knot friendship wristbands, make sure you choose a material other than wool. If wool gets in touch with water, it can get matted very quickly. And be honest, you don't want that to happen, do you?

Cashmere

This material is highly water-resistant, soft and lightweight, tear-proof and likewise breathable. The only downside of Cashmere is that it belongs to the most expensive textiles of the world.

Sisal

Whosoever has been into the traditional Macrame art, will be aware of the fact that especially Sisal is one of the most-used materials. Since having a good thickness, people prefer to use it for more complex projects. Apart from that, it's highly tear-proof. However, somebody with sensitive hands should be wearing safety gloves when working with Sisal yarn. It's very scratchy, would strain the skin of the hands and could even be the cause of injuries. If you buy Sisal, you should in any case watch out for the length being on sale. Since it's very thick, Sisal is mostly offered for sale in portions with a length of about 1o to 15 centimetres only.

Jute

The origins of Jute are to be found in Bangladesh. It's very decay-proof, for which reason it can be easily used for outdoor decorations. Another positive property of Jute is that it's hardly fuzzing, and the skin won't be irritated that much. Because of its specific impregnation, Jute is made for all weather conditions. If you wish to use a thicker jute rope, you must know that its elasticity is rather low. Jute can be purchased in every DIY store.

Paracord

This yarn is made of artificial threads with a very smooth surface. You can even buy it multi-coloured. It's very robust and is therefore the ideal choice for knotting friendship wristbands. Some Macrame enthusiasts also use Paracord as a fashion yarn.

Leather Straps

These straps are also highly appreciated for Macrame use. If knotting is over, it's easy to make out the minute details on the straps. Unfortunately, leather straps are available in predefined sizes only. If you wish to buy bigger rolls, you better consult Amazon. But watch out for the length on offer.

Further Materials

I'm really happy to proclaim good news to you here: Using Macrame, you can let go freely all your creativity and imagination, since everything is possible. Whether simple pearls or mother-of-pearl from the DIY store – you can use everything to set fabulous accents and even create sounds. You only have to make sure that the material you picked for your project fits in size to the knotting thread you use. If you use a very thin species of yarn, it will firstly look strange when placing a big mother-of-pearl on it; and, secondly, it wouldn't have any firm hold, and you would be running the risk that your project would get broken soon.

Some of the materials which are very often used for knotting projects I wish to explain to you in more detail:

Wooden pearls

These pearls are probably the most widely used deco material for knotting projects. You can find them in different forms, colours and sizes and will always get something fitting for your purposes. Wooden pearls are manufactured from various woods, about which you will learn more in Chapter 14.1.

But also glass-like acrylic pearls are being more and more used for Macrame projects. The upside is that they are less expensive and much more robust than wooden pearls. You can also find these pearls in all possible colours, forms and sizes.

Feathers

Particularly, if you wish to create dream-catchers, feathers should never be missing. They add the proper charm to the piece of jewellery you're making. In the case of traditional dream-catchers, as the Indians used to make them, eagle feathers play an important role because the eagle is a symbol of the connection between heaven and earth.

White feathers symbolize protection, brown feathers stand for health and black feathers are said to mitigate grief, while grey feathers are a symbol of peace. You see, even feathers are significant. I will give you more details on the different feathers you can use in Chapter 14.

Objects that create sound

Lovely sounds that contribute to our finding inner peace can also be wonderfully integrated into your Macrame projects. What about a Macrame wind chime? You can knot these wind chimes like dream-catchers, use pearls instead of feathers and choose small bells and tone bars. If you want to have something less expensive, you can convert coasters and integrate them into your Macrame project.

Did you know that the wind chime itself is very old? The origins of this wonderful musical highlight can be traced back to the 8th and 12th century. In those days the soothsayers claimed to foresee the future when listening to the lovely sound of a wind chime. People used wind chimes for their front doors, where they served as a means of protection against evil spirits.

Generally speaking, Japan is considered to be the place where wind chimes came from. They can be manufactured with different materials like shells, which symbolize protection and prosperity. But they are also a symbol of fertility. Apart from that, there is bamboo, which stands for growth and longevity. Bells you can use have an inviting effect. Metal and glass, symbolizing descendants and relationships, are widely used, too.

Let's have a closer look at the word "mobile". The word is originally French and denotes a hanging object. As soon as it is set in motion by air, nice sounds are created. If you wish to make such a wind chime, you can proceed like making a dream-catcher, the only difference being that you need four cords for hanging it up. Then, for example, the ring with the hanging tone bars, can function like a plate.

Clasps

Whosoever wishes to create Macrame jewellery must also take care of the proper means of closure. It might be rather easy in case of a friendship wristband because it's simply knotted around the wrist of the arm. But if you wish to make nice pieces of fashion jewellery, you should use lobster clasps, magnetic clasps or rings.

The Thickness of the Material

You can buy ropes with a length from 1.5 mm to 6 mm in every DIY shop. But always remember that the thicker the rope you're using, the more rustic the look of the material. If you wish to produce jewellery, you should take ropes that are less thick.

How to calculate the length of the thread

There is no general formula for calculating the length of a thread. The actual length you need always depends on the kind of knots you plan to use for your project. In case of a reef knot, for example, the working cords need to be a bit longer than the middle cords since you need them for making several wraps around the middle cords.

If you wish to make simple knots and your pieces of Macrame jewellery is supposed to have a length of 20 cm, you must multiply the length by four. So, your cords should have a minimum length of 80 cm. As for myself, I used to take threads which are a few centimetres longer than needed in order to be on the safe side. Now, it's really easy to find out how many cords you need: The total of the cords should always be divisible by four because certain knots can only be made with four cords.

Further stuff you need

Without tools at your disposal, you simply won't get anywhere. But, let me tell you at this point that there aren't very many tools you should have.

Macrame-Scissors

If you buy a pair of scissors you need for your Macrame projects, bear in mind that it has to be fitting to the thickness of the yarn you take. Since the yarn itself may have varying diameters, I recommend you get yourself scissors with different sizes, which will enable you to apply clean and orderly cuts.

Tape measure

Most people have got rulers with a maximum length of 30 cm at home. So if you consider the use of a ruler too awkward, you can buy a tape measure instead. This tape is flexible and easier to handle with its length of two meters than a 30 cm ruler. The disadvantage about a ruler like that is that, additionally, you will have to calculate how often the yarn ends must be joined to get the length you need.

Support

For some projects you might need more than a clipboard or a duct tape. In case of larger objects, it can be very helpful to hang them up on the back of a chair, on the door or on cupboards. The length and variety of the cords may easily cause them to get tangled up, and you end up having double work.

Gloves

Some threads, Sisal for example, make it necessary to work with gloves to protect your skin. Working with this material and touching it all the time, has enormous irritating effects on your skin and, in worst cases, can even cause serious injuries.

Comb

Certain Macrame projects require the rope to be frayed as a final step. That works best, if you comb out the yarn. Then, everything will be even.

Hairspray or straightening iron

In order to stabilize the frayed-out threads of a feather or of an angel (both projects will be explained later in this book), you can use hairspray to fix them. If you don't wish to use hairspray because of its strong smell, you may use a straightening iron instead. But be careful! It gets hots very quickly and using it too long may cause the threads to burn.

Great! Now you've learned the most important basics of Macrame

and are ready to start off with your first projects.

So, that things won't be too challenging for you in the beginning,

I chose to make you acquainted with easy projects first.

I wish you all the best for your work and much fun trying out Macrame.

Perhaps you will soon become a full-time Macrame enthusiast and be tying and knotting all the time.

Chapter 6
Lanyard Keychain

A lanyard keychain, manufactured by means of a wonderful knotting technique and having a charming pattern, is something rare. So, your keychain will soon be a true eye-catcher for your friends, acquaintances, family members and other people you meet.

Lanyard keychains are particularly suitable as a personal gift, all the more when being handmade.

And here's how you're getting to your personal lanyard keychain:

Materials

- Scissors
- Tape measure
- Duct tape
- Keychain
- Yarn
- Comb
- Macrame-cords
  (three to five mm)

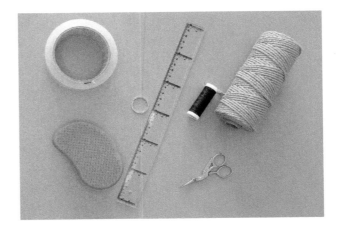

1

Choose one or more colours you like, and you want to use. Cut to measure four cords. They should have a length of 120 cm.

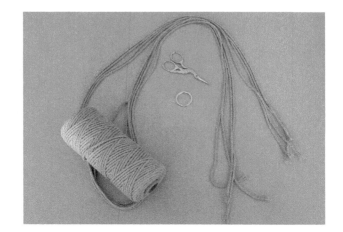

2

Take the duct tape and fix the keychain to the table or to a pad, so it can't move while you work.

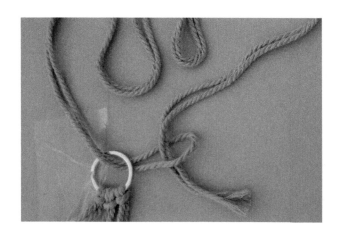

3

Then double the threads which are to be fixed to the ring as follows: Pass the loop through the ring. Then feed the loose ends into the loop and tighten the cord fast to the ring. Repeat that with the other cords as well.

4

Now you've got eight cords in front of you. Then separate them in the middle so that you have four cords on each side. The cords in the middle are your working cords.

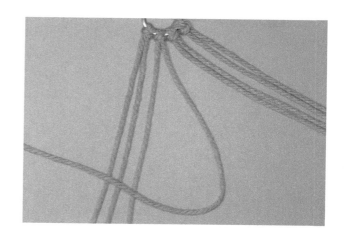

5

Let's start on the left side while you put the four cords on the right side aside for now. Place your working cord over the three other cords in such as manner as to produce a loop.

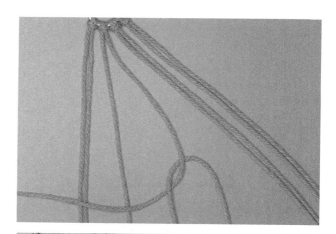

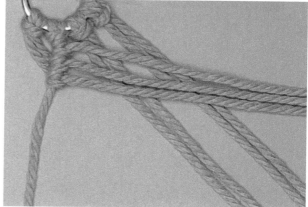

6

Proceed with the other cord. Knot it around the working cord two times. Pass the first cord over and under the working cord and then bring it through the loop. Then move the finished knot up. Repeat this step with the first cord.

7

Repeat step 6) with the second and third cord, too. In the end, you must have six finished knots on your working cord.

8

Now repeat the whole procedure with the right side. Always remember: Two times over, under, through per cord.

9

Then put the outermost cords on each side aside. You don't need them for the next step. Now, the focus is on the four middle cords. Then make a reef knot around the middle cords. First, place the right cord over the four middle cords and under the left cord.

10

Then pull out the left cord from under the right cord and under the four middle cords, and then over the right cord. Repeat this step to the other side. Then, carefully, pull both knots tight.

11

Now repeat steps 5) and 6) using three cords to make double knots on the working cords.

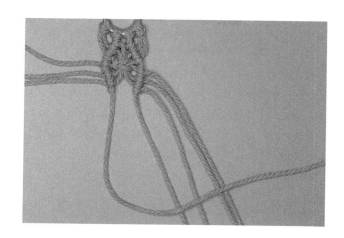

12

Let's come to the complicated steps: Continue knotting the left knot-row to the lower right side. It's not that hard because, basically, you proceed as before, only that you knot the cords (6,7 and 8) of the right side over your left working knot. Seen from left, the fifth cord becomes your working cord, you now take to continue knotting under the left row to the left in order to knot the rows together in a criss-cross manner.

13

Now, it's time for the reef knot from steps 9) and 10). From here onwards, all steps will have to be repeated. Depending on the length, the pattern can be repeated three times.

14

Pull the knot of the last row a bit tighter and cut the cords to measure with your scissors, as you please. You can also take some yarn and tie the ends together to obtain a tassel. That's entirely up to your personal taste.

Chapter 7
Lantern for placing

Especially in summer when you're having a nice BBQ in your garden or when there's a festivity, lanterns are a real eye-catcher. You can create that special effect, if you choose to make use of Macrame techniques. There are several patterns and possibilities to cover the glass of lanterns with enchanting knots.

How that works and what you need to create such effects, you will learn in the following step-by-step instructions.

Materials

- Empty honey glass
- DIY Jute cord with a length of 40 m and a thickness of 2 mm
- Pair of scissors
- Tea lights
- Hot glue

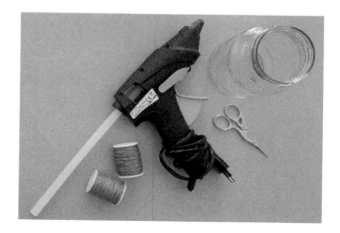

1

Wrap your Jute cord several times around the upper rim of the glass. Then tie both ends together.

2

Cut to measure another cord which should be a bit longer than the glass and double it. Pass the loop through the cord already fixed. Then move the ends of the new cord through the loop and pull everything tight. Depending on the dimensions of the glass, you repeat this procedure with other cords. But make sure they're equidistant.

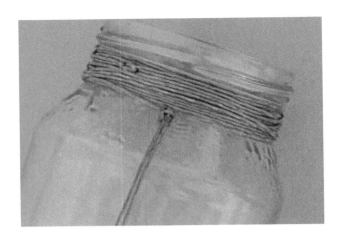

3

There are two cords lying next to each other per knot, right? Take the cord on the right side of the first knot and then the cord on the left side of the second knot. Tie both together. Repeat this around the entire glass.

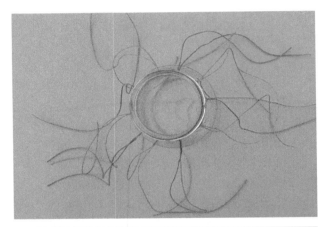

4

Now, there should always be two new cords next to each other. Proceed as explained above. Tie the right cord of the first knot to the left cord of the second knot and continue until you've got a net enveloping your glass.

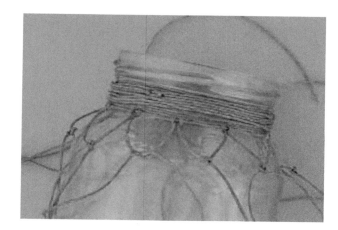

5

Turn your glass upside down for continuing with its bottom. Then take hot glue and fix the ends of all cords to the bottom of the glass. And, hey, your fisher-net lantern is already finished! Turn it around again, place your tea light inside and light it when evening has come. You will see how cosy and decorative such a lantern can be.

Chapter 8
Lantern for Hanging up

Not only do lanterns for placing look charming, but they're also as charming when hanging. They're suitable for a nice garden party or a beautiful living accessory. Just have a look at the step-by-step instructions I'm providing below, and you will realize how easy it is to copy this wonderful Macrame pattern.

Materials

- Jam pot
- Parcel string or Macrame yarn
- Pair of scissors
- Wire (perhaps)
- Decorative stuff for inside (sand, tea light, shells, reeds)

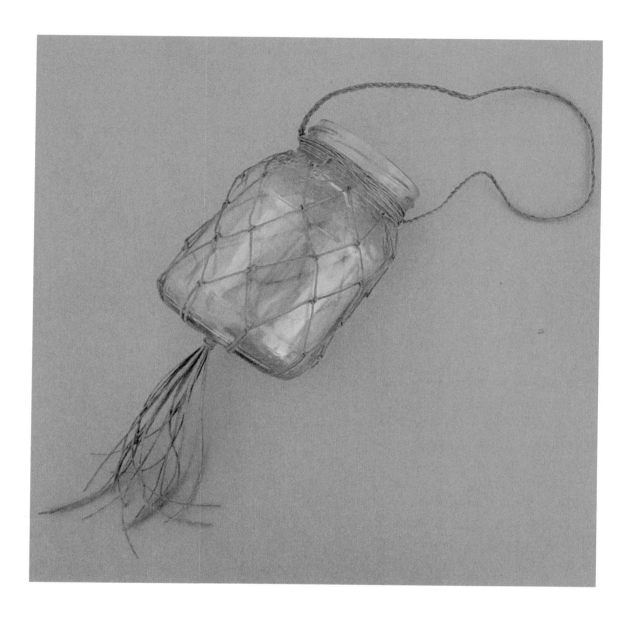

1

Wrap your DIY Jute cord several times around the upper rim of the glass. Important: Both ends must be long enough to be later used as a handle. Then wrap another cord around the rim of the glass. Proceed as explained above. In the end, you will have obtained four cords which make a stable handle.

2

Cut to measure a second cord which should be a bit longer than your glass and double it. Pass the loop through the cord already fixed. The ends of the new cord are moved through the loop and pulled tight. Depending on the dimensions of the glass, you repeat this step with other cords. Make sure they're equidistant.

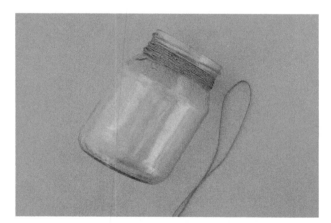

3

There are two cords lying next to each other per knot, right? Take the cord on the right side of the first knot and then the cord on the left side of the second knot. Tie both together. Repeat this around the entire glass.

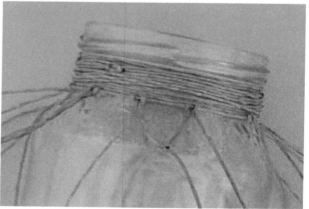

4

Now, there should always be two new cords next to each other. Proceed as explained above. Tie the right cord of the first knot to the left cord of the second knot and continue until you've got a net enveloping your glass.

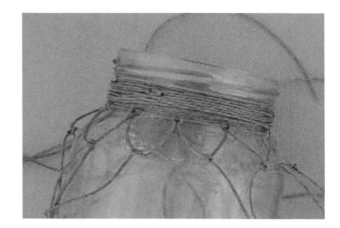

5

Turn your glass upside down to continue with its bottom. Continue tying knots until there is no more yarn left. Then wrap another cord around all other cord ends so that you obtain a nice tassel. Alternatively, you can use a beautiful big pearl though which the ends of the cords are passed and tightened. Or you tie them together to make one simple knot which is to be pushed up.

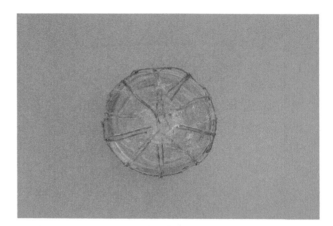

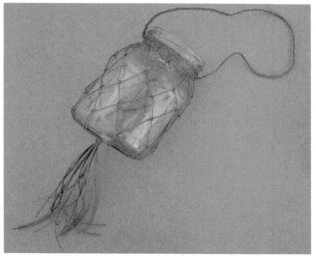

Chapter 9
Key-Ring

Everybody can buy a key-ring – but not everybody can manufacture it. All you need are threads, the proper knot and the right enthusiasm to become a creator. In the following you find simple step-by-step instructions to self-made such a key-ring. Have a lot of fun!

Materials

- Clipboard
- Ruler
- Key-ring
- Comb
- Macrame yarn in a colour of your choice

1

Choose two colours for your key-ring and cut two cords to measure. They should have a length of 60 cm.

2

Double the cords and move the loop through the key-ring. Then pull the loose ends through the loop, making sure that the cords are pulled tight to the key-ring.

3

Put the two outermost cords aside, that is to the left and to the right. First, we're knotting the lanyard, for which purpose we're making a carrick bend. Take the left cord and place it over the middle cords in such a manner as to form an L.

4

First move the right cord over the L, then under the middle cords and pass it through the loop of the L-cord. Then pull everything tight. Now you repeat the carrick bend on the right side, which means you're working back-to-front.

5

Make the lanyard as long as possible. Having reached its end, you move the lower end up to the key-ring so that you obtain a double lanyard. Then cut to measure a new short cord.

6

Place one end of the new cord in such a manner as to be slightly longer than your key-ring. Take the other end, make a loop and wrap it around the double lanyard several times.

7

Pass the end of the cord through the loop and hold fast. Pull at its upper end, which should be protruding from the wrap. As by magical hands, the knot under the wrap will disappear.

8

Then shorten the cords, so everything looks orderly. And, hey, your key-ring is already finished.

Chapter 10
Coaster

Somebody is coming for a coffee to you, and you wish to present something out of the ordinary? What about a Macrame coaster for cups, plates or other items? Depending on the length of your threads, you can magically create wonderful pieces of art. Have a look at the step-by-step instructions I'm giving below and take a crack at your first coaster with several knots.

Materials

- Cork plate
- Pins
- Pair of scissors
- Macrame yarn
- Ruler
- Comb

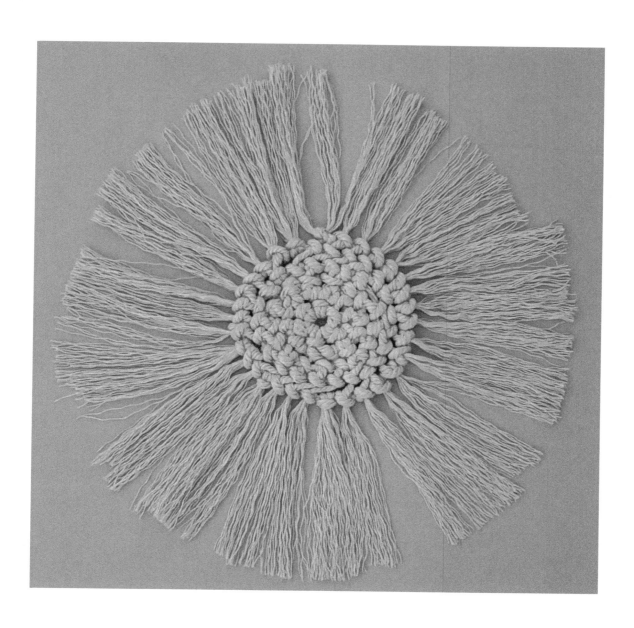

1

Cut to measure the cords you want to work with. They need to have the following measures: one cord 180 cm, five cords 85 cm and some other cords about 60 cm.

2

Choose the longest cord as your main thread. Place it as a loop on your working pad. Make sure that one end of the cord is longer than the other, since this one will become your main thread in a later step. Then fix the five threads with a length of 85 cm to the main thread by means of a half turn.

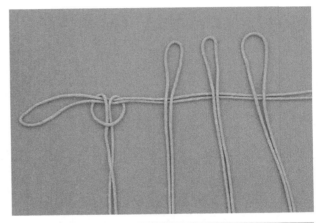

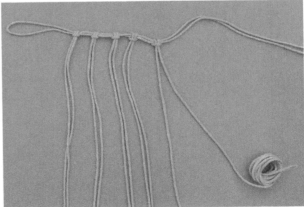

3

Move the five cords tightly together. Then pass the loose end of your main thread though the loop and pull it tight. Together with the ends of the main thread the five cords become a flower, so to speak, whose knots are forming its interior.

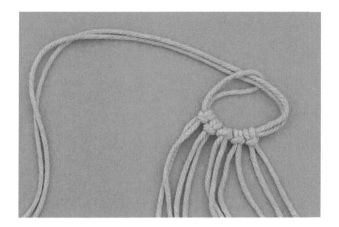

4

Then take pins and fix the circle to your cork plate in order to create a support for your future coaster.

5

Move the cord next to your main thread under it, pass it over and again under it. Then tighten the cord. You best have a closer look at the images. They are helpful. Repeat this step with the same cord to finally get a full turn.

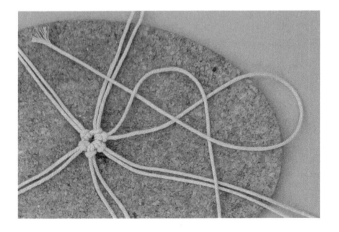

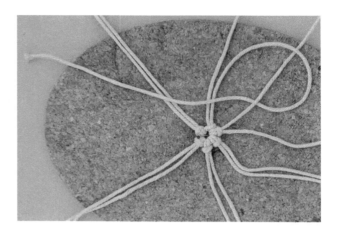

6

Repeat this step with the other cords and only stop when they're becoming too short. Caution: Sometimes wider gaps are created in the process. In order to fill them up, fix the cords with the length of 60 cm to your main thread.

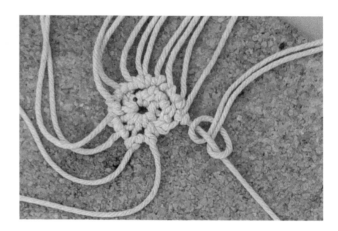

7

Having reached the end, you tie the main thread to the nearest cord. You will be having a coaster with radiating ends in front of you now. Then comb them.

8

Take a pair of scissors and trim the fringes to the desired length. As a kind of support and for making sure everything be straight in the end, you can place a round plate on a coaster and cut off the protruding fringes.

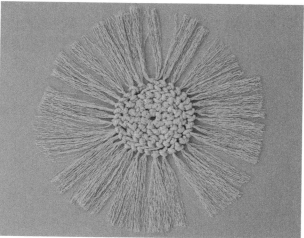

Chapter 11
Dummy Chain

What about a self-made dummy chain for your baby? Perhaps there is offspring among your friends, and you wish to convince them with a DIY-gift? If yes, this is the right place to be. In the following, I'm presenting to you two easy-to-copy variants.

Materials

- Macrame yarn
- Pendant
- (Dummy) clip with image
- Pair of scissors
- Tape measure or ruler

1

Cut your yarn to measure as follows:

- 2 x 90 cm
- 1 x 200 cm
- 2 x 40 cm

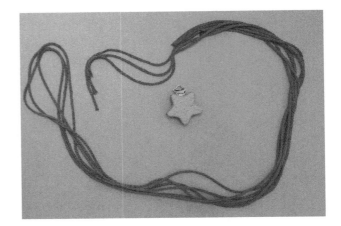

2

Take the 90 cm cords, form a loop and fix it to the clip by means of an anchor knot. Do the same with the 200 cm cord. Now, you've got a total of six cords hanging from the clip.

3

Divide the six cords in the middle and place the cords on the right side aside, so they can't be bothering you. We start off with the left side, that is, with a carrick bend. Two cords are placed in the middle and one on either side of the far left and far right.

4

Take the left cord, place it L-shaped over the middle cords and under the right cord on the far right. Take the right cord, bring it under the L-cord and the middle cords, so it can be passed up again inside the L-loop. Pull your half carrick bend tight and repeat the whole procedure, however, this time you start off with the cord on the right side. Proceed as described, only back-to-front.

5

Put the knotted cords aside and take the other cords. Add to these the two right cords on the left side, so you can work with a total of four cords. Apart from that, the mesh is tied together in this manner.

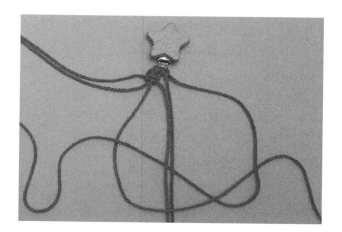

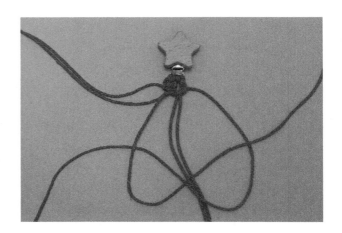

6

Make a carrick bend on the right side. Afterwards, you divide the cords in order to be able to make another carrick bend on the left side. Proceed with these steps and stop after you achieve the desired length for your chain.

7

To give your chain the finishing touch, you place all cords in a such a manner as to have four middle cords. The two outer cords are used to make a carrick bend.

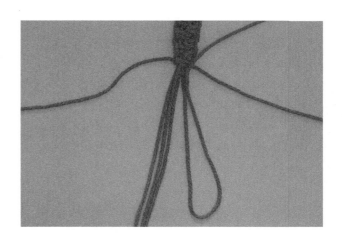

8

Take a 40 cm cord and place it as a loop to the end of the chain. Then take the second one and proceed as follows: One end of the cord must be placed in such a manner as to protrude over the most recently made carrick bend. Take the other end and bend it into a loop. Then make wraps around the loop and the cords. Bring the end of the cord through the loop and hold fast with one hand. With your other hand you pull at the upper end of the cord. That's called winding knot. This is a good trick to hide the knot completely under the wrap.

9

Then cut the ends of the band to their proper measure and fix the key-ring to the loop, so the dummy can be attached to it later. Or you fix it to the loop straight away without using a key-ring as a support.

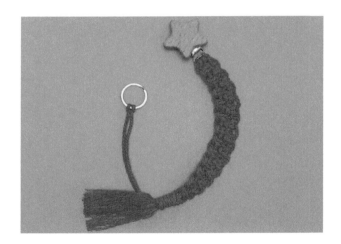

Second Variant:

Alternatively, you can make the chain with a wave knot for which purpose you make a carrick bend. However, you're not supposed to double it, but use but one side of it. Doing so, you obtain a spiral-like band which you may complete with a winding knot.

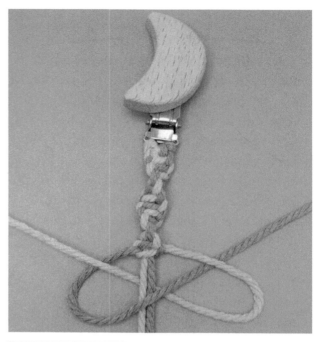

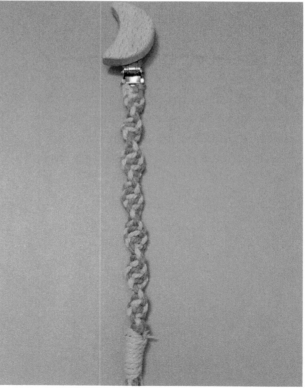

Chapter 12
Feather

Feathers are so wonderful and are very suitable as wall decoration or as table ornaments. Using Macrame, you can create great feathers. I'm showing you how you're supposed to proceed.

Materials

- Macrame yarn white (but you can also create multi-coloured feathers)
- Pair of scissors
- Comb
- Ruler, tape measure

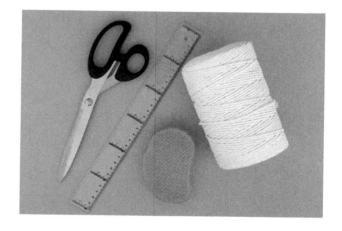

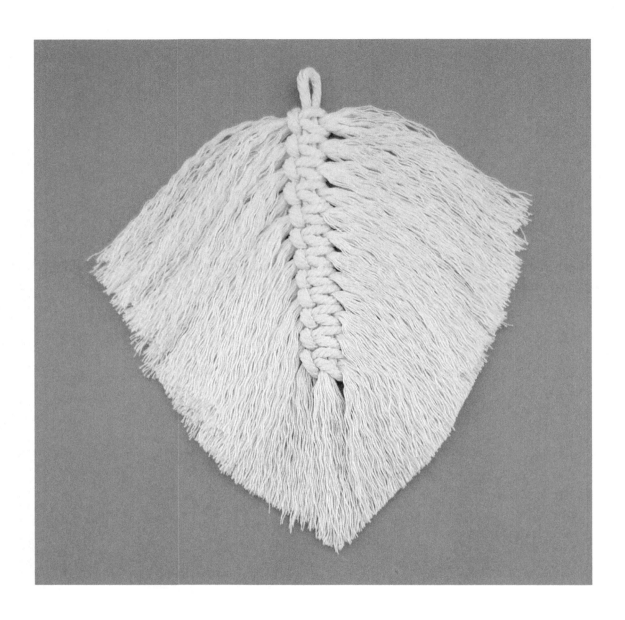

Step-by-step Instructions

1

Cut to measure a cord with a length of 30 cm and 24 cords with a length of 20 cm. If you wish to have a larger feather, you need shorter cords and also choose a greater length for all of your cords.

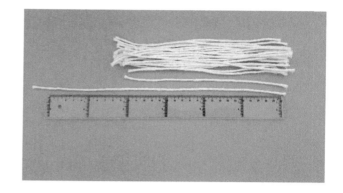

2

The longer cord must be placed as an upright loop on your work pad.

3

Take the first shorter cord and bend it into a loop. Then move it under your main thread.

4

Take the second shorter cord, which you bend into a loop, too. Then stick the loose ends of the second cord through the loop of the first cord. Pass the loose ends of the first cord through the loop of the second cord.

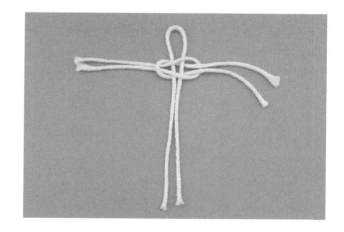

5

Pull both cords tight, making sure it's not too tight. Otherwise, the cords can slip over the loop of your main thread. You need them later for hanging up your feather.

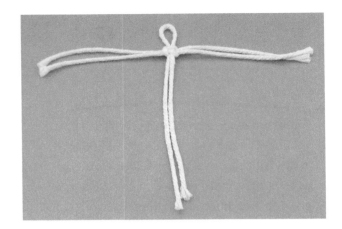

6

Repeat these steps with the remaining cords. Always take two cords which you tie to the main thread. If there's no cord left, tie the ends of the main thread together.

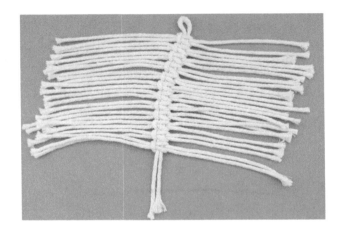

7

Now comb the ends of the cords. Advice: If you wish to have combed-out cords with a smooth surface, you can take a straightening iron or regular iron.

8

Trim the fringes into the form you wish for your feather. Then carefully cut them to fit.

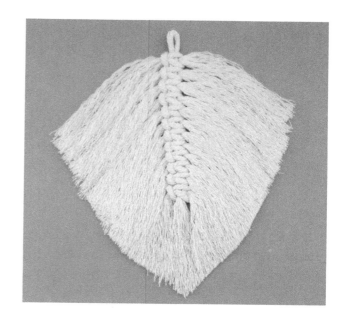

9

Then place your feather on a sheet of paper and apply hairspray, thus making sure that its form remains in place.

Chapter 13
Friendship Wristband

It's a ritual that will never go lost. A friendship is sealed with a band which has the same shape and colours. There are uncountable possibilities to create such a band. For your first band I'm presenting a set of simple instructions and wish you all success in copying it.

Materials

- Macrame yarn in different colours (thin)
- Ruler or tape measure
- Clipboard
- Pair of scissors

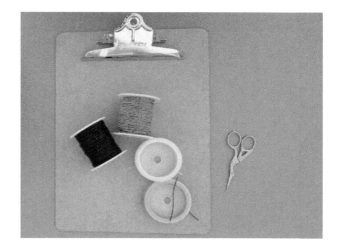

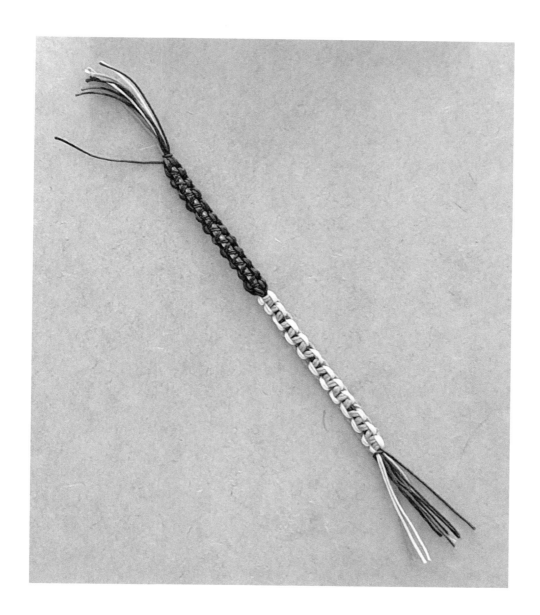

1

Cut four cords to measure, which should have a minimum length of 80 cm. Then tie them together well.

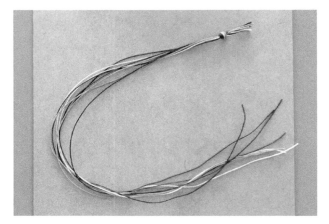

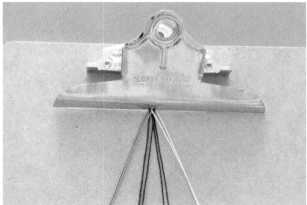

2

In order to add more stability, pin everything to a clipboard.

3

I chose the carrick bend for my friendship wristband. It's the knot I like best. Separate the two outermost cords from the rest. Take the left cord and form it into an L over the middle cords. Pass the right cord over the left cord and then under it and the middle cords. Move this one up again in the L-loop and pull everything tight. Repeat these steps back-to-front on the right side.

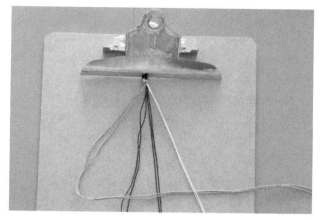

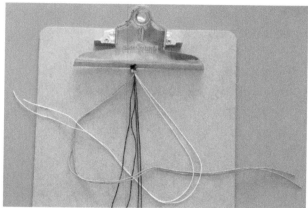

4

Continue with the carrick bend and stop when the cords have become too short. You can also swap the cords in such as manner as to enable you to start off with the right cord to make it into a carrick bend at about half-length. Make sure that the colours you use are not the same to achieve a result as seen in the image. By the way, I doubled the cord, since the yarn I used was rather thin. You can either take a thicker yarn or create a thin wristband.

5

Then take the end and make it into a knot. Now, your wristband is ready for use. Or you can close up the end with a wrap knot.

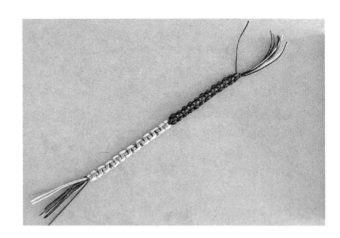

Second Variant:

If you have made a certain number of car-rick bends, you may add pearls to your piece of art. The pearls are pushed on two middle cords. Then, you proceed as before.

Chapter 14
Colours

Colours – there are so many of them. Well, that's at least what we suppose when looking at a colour palette. Actually, there are only three basic colours: Red, blue and yellow. Basic colours are those colours which you can't produce by mixing two other colours. They are also called primary colours.

If you mix the basic colours, you obtain so-called secondary colours or second level colours. Among them are counted green, orange, purple. If you wish to go one step further and mix primary and secondary colours, you obtain the so-called tertiary colours. One example for a tertiary colour is the mix of blue (basic colour) and green (primary colour). Depending on the colour portion, you obtain a soft bluish green (tertiary colour).

But there are more colour categories than these three: You can also ascribe to them properties and meanings which assume great importance in the art of Macrame.

Did you know that there even is a colour therapy? For example, take a look at the bath salts you use. They don't only have pleasant smells, but also are coloured in such a way as to be fitting to the ethereal oils they contain.

Let's have a look at the best-known colours. You will see that it's a highly interesting subject and that the choice of the colour for your yarn can really tip the scales.

Red corresponds to the colour of fire and is thought to be symbolical of love and passion. This colour is also often equated with anger and wrath (see emoji's). In any case, the red colour provokes attention and is indicative of energy and vitality. So, the colour red is able to heat up, activate and make hot. It can even speed up our metabolism and circulatory system. People wearing red clothes often symbolize their self-confidence without being aware of it. Red dresses make women look hot, and loud red clothes attract people's attention. Whosoever wishes to use this colour for rooms (colour, furniture), should be warned to use it economically. Otherwise, if there's too much of this colour, we can get restless. Hush! Special advice: If love is supposed to be kindled, it's worth-while to wear red clothes. It makes passionate and stimulates the partner's appetite.

Orange is symbolical of zest for life and optimism. This colour brightens up your mood and indicates openness, self-confidence and sociability. Sometimes this colour also conveys obtrusiveness or happy-go-lucky nature. If your stomach or lower abdomen hurts, you should go into the problems right away. The colour orange can be helpful in the process of mitigating such symptoms because it has uplifting effects. It can even promote the function of your kidneys.

Wearing orange-coloured clothes can intensify your personal attraction. If you're in places where the walls are painted orange, it doesn't take long for you to get into a sociable mood. This colour has truly inviting and promoting effects, turning rooms into cosy places. As a rule, you can say that kitchens don't get much daylight. That's why shades of orange are very suitable to brighten up these rooms.

Yellow is the colour of light, of the sun, optimism and joy. This colour has the wonderful property to mitigate of fears and depressions. Shades of yellow are chosen to treat liver issues, rheumatism and a weakened immune system. It has detoxing effects.

A clear yellow colour is symbolical of reason, logic and knowledge, whereas the dirty yellow colours usually stand for stinginess, jealousy or egoism. Whosoever likes to wear yellow outfits, symbolizes zest for life and self-confidence.

Small rooms appear bigger when shades of yellow are used. If you want to promote the mental concentration and the creativity of your child, you should pick a yellow colour for painting the children's room. That also applies to conference rooms.

Green is symbolical of nature, hope and safety. It has calming and harmonizing effects. People who suffer from cardiac diseases are often treated with a colour therapy and, particularly, with green colours. They contribute to mitigating lovesickness, anger or grief.

Sometimes the green colour also conveys feelings like weariness, envy or indifference. People wearing green clothes appear particularly trustworthy and generous. If green is used in rooms, it serves to provide a sense of safety, creativity and calm. Therefore, it's the best colour for rooms in which people are supposed to work. Often, green plants or green accessories serve the purpose (Macrame wall hangings)

Turquoise is a cool and fresh colour which indicates mental openness and freedom. But it can also have distancing effects. This colour is used in case of infections and all sorts of allergies in order to protect the immune system. People wearing turquoise outfits appear extravagant and extraordinary. Rooms pained in turquoise have a cool but also very personal appearance.

Blue is symbolical of calm, longing and trust. Our sky is blue. Sometimes the colour blue appears careless, indifferent and melancholic. People who suffer from insomnia should integrate blue colours in their sleeping form. Blue is a colour that is helpful in case of inflammatory diseases. It has promoting effects on our linguistic abilities and our clear thinking. People wearing blue outfits know exactly what they want in life. Often, they appear very cool. If you want to make a small room appear bigger, you should choose to paint it blue. Rooms that are painted blue to add a sense of relaxation are exactly what you should be going for.

Purple is symbolical of dignity, protection and mysticism. It is extravagant, has mitigating, purging and even purifying effects. Purple is the colour of art and the inspirations connected with it. People wearing purple clothes can appear proud, but also arrogant. But this colour is also festive, noble and even mysterious. Likewise, it has supporting effects on your mental concentration and self-confidence. If you choose shades of purple for your home, it has calming effects. However, purple is better suited for reception rooms. Never use purple in your bedroom or dining room. Why? It restrains your appetite and lust for bodily affection and tenderness.

Magenta, Pink, Rose are the natural colours expressing joy. Both are soft and express orderliness, empathy and idealism. At the same time, they even have certain egoistic aspects. Magenta is used in cases of medical emergencies, since it's understood to be a protective colour. It makes you feel inner peace and also conveys safety.

Pink clothes are considered to be very expressive, whereas rose-coloured clothes appear innocent. Experts take the view that pink would be the ideal colour for bedrooms, since it can serve to reduce aggression.

White – thinking of hospitals, we know that this colour is standing for purity. Likewise, it is symbolical of clearness and innocence. It's the colour of ice and snow and therefore expresses aloofness. White is counted among the magical colours. It can be used for every other colour. Having a look at its light spectrum, you soon realize that it contains almost all existing colours. In China it is considered to be a dream-colour and even the colour of death. In this country, however, you don't find any negative associations with it. People dressing up in white, appear elegant, but can appear unapproachable at the same time. As far as rooms as concerned, it's perfect for colour combinations because of its brightening, invigorating and neutralizing effects.

Grey is symbolical of complete neutrality and reticence. But people also associate the colour grey with boredom, insecurity and fear of life. Apart from that, it appears unobtrusive. Some gents like wearing grey business suits because they appear sober and rational and conceal individuality. If you want to use the colour grey, always choose combinations with other colours.

Black stands for darkness. In this country, the colour black is expressive of grief and unfathomableness. At the same time, black is symbolical of dignity and esteem. If you wear black clothes, you appear serious and produce a sense of respect in other people.

Brown is a quiet earthen colour that conveys comfort and material safety. The brown colour is used in colour therapy for people suffering from vertigo. Also, brown is considered to be a trendy business colour. Rooms with a dominating brown appear rustic, calming and balancing. You can use ochre and sienna in nearly all kinds of rooms.

Gold is a colour that is very often related to the sun. It stands for wealth and power, gives you strength and inspirations. Apart from that, gold is helpful against insecurity, fear and indifference. Thinking of the golden wedding, we know that gold is likewise the colour of jubilees. It is a quiet virtue, just as loyalty and friendship, truth and helpfulness.

Silver has purging and harmonizing effects. It promotes communication, but also largely promotes dishonesty and talkativeness. Silver is the colour of politeness, astuteness, independence, security and punctuality.

It has a beautiful shine and is thus a mirror for other colours, that is, in such a pure manner as to become a background colour itself. The colour silver is symbolical of anything modern, unconventional and original.

14.1 Wood – Properties and Effects

If you belong to those people who wish to add to their Macrame projects a certain extraordinary flair and some kind of unique style, you can count on the different types of wood at your disposal. These types of wood wonderfully complete your project when combined with the fitting colours. In contrast to stone and metal, it is one of the qualities of wood to have relaxing effects. Thinking of the American Indians and having a closer look at their Macrame skills, we soon become aware of that fact, all the more they used to work a lot with natural materials like wood.

Metal and concrete are considered to be linear and if you ever fell on a concrete ground, you will have experienced its very hardness. Due to its soothing and relaxing effects, wood is able to make us feel better, for which reason it is very often used for interior design purposes. And it doesn't matter, if it's used for a piece of furniture or as decoration in the form of figures or for Macrame projects.

For many years wood was replaced by white walls and white furniture, but there are studies in support of the fact that people are more and more longing for getting back to nature, and that's why wood has become a trendy material for interior design use again.

Did you know that wood absorbs only smallest amounts of UV light? The effect on our eyes is that they won't get tired that quickly.

Before you start off with using wood for your Macrame projects, I recommend you get more detailed information on that subject.

It can well be said that wood types with expressive structure are considered peaceful and warm. Types of wood with a parallel structure contribute to a relaxed feeling in the room. If you choose dark wood, the room appears cosy and protective. Light wood, on the other hand, makes a room appear bigger than it really is.

Tip: As a rule, a dark-brown colour should be mainly used for furniture. It's otherwise a very unpleasant sight.

Let's have a more detailed look at the various types of wood available:

Ash, Maple and Linden

These three tree-species belong to the light wood types. If you combine these types with pastel shades or light-blue, you create calming effects.

Birch

Birch is a light wood, which we can see from the birch trunk with its white shine. As its bark is rather unique, birchwood can be wonderfully used for wall hangings. If you are familiar with the Swedish interior design, you will know that birch is often combined with shades of light-blue and yellow.

Oak

Oak wood has a very strong structure to enchant us, which is the reason why it's so widely appreciated. It's interesting that though its wood is tan-coloured, it's counted among the dark wood types. You can combine oak wood with a great variety of colours in wonderful ways. It's peculiar to oak wood that it won't become pale even after years of use.

Walnut and Cherry

People who wish to work with white Macrame yarn should in any case combine it with the dark, red-brown type of wood from these two trees. Using it, you can produce a read eye-catcher and create a real explosion of colours. By the way, it's a wonderful idea to combine the wood of the walnut tree with claret.

Beech

Beech has got a very close-structure type of wood, for which reason it can be easily differentiated from other trees. Due to its slightly reddish to medium-brown colour, it is counted among the dark types of wood. You can easily combine beech wood with various shades of white or grey.

Coniferous Trees

Basically, it can be said that the wood of coniferous trees is rather light. Particularly, the fir tree has got a very distinct and enduring smell which is very appreciated by many people. The downside of this type of wood, however, is that it secretes great amounts of resin very quickly, for which reason it should be de-resined prior to use. Also, it's fairly difficult to colour it. People who wish to use wood from coniferous trees can get hold of it in DIY shops. The wood you can buy there is definitely pre-treated in the best of ways.

Chapter 15
Mandala

They have become part of our life. When we were kids, we would often colour or design them ourselves. The meaning of the word "Mandala" is "circle or circular in shape". The outer circles are symmetrical and surround the centre point, which is called Bindu. Bindu is thought to symbolize the mythical Mountain of the Universe. Have a look at these easy instructions I'm giving you. You can also use knots for creating wonderful mandalas. I've picked a simple motif for your first steps in making mandalas.

Materials

- Macrame yarn
- Ruler
- Ring (at least 20 cm)
- Pair of scissors
- Clipboard

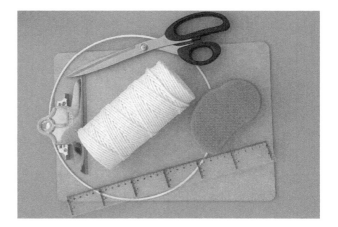

1

First, you cut to measure 40 cords with
a length of at least 30 cm. I recommend
extending the length to 35 or 40 cm,
since the knots make the cords shorter.
Also, it's fairly difficult to make the surrounding part of the mandala when using short cords.

2

With an anchor knot you fix four of
these cords to your ring. You should
have eight strands hanging down from
it in the end. Take four of these hanging
cords and tie them into carrick bend.
Then repeat this step with the other
four strands as well. Now you've got
eight strands, each of them forming a
carrick bend. Tie them together. Then
push together two of these knots and
put aside the outermost cords on the
left and right side. There are now four
cords in the middle, which you also tie
into a carrick bend. Now, all of your
strands are tied up with each other. If
you look at your carrick bend mesh,
you will see that they're appearing like
small triangles.

3

Repeat these steps until all of your cords are fixed to the ring and no more triangles can be made. Now fix a cord between all of these triangles by means of an anchor knot, so you obtain two working strands again.

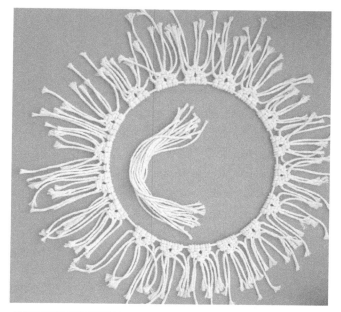

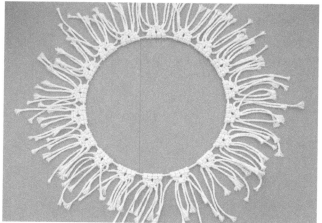

4

It's time for your clove hitch. Place one of the new working strands L-shaped over the cords of the triangles. This is your anchor knot, around which the working cords are wrapped. Caution! In case of a clove hitch, each working cord must be doubled.

5

Proceed like that on the left side of the triangle and stop when both anchor knots meet below. Then fix everything with a normal knot. Repeat steps 4) and 5) until all of your triangles have nice surrounding parts. But you can also leave them out, as I did.

6

Comb the remaining cords as good as you can. Then you can trim them into the right form with a pair of scissors.

7

If you wish to design the middle part of your mandala, you can work with thin Macrame yarn. You proceed working with the cord like you usually do when making a dream-catcher. Please see the instructions in chapter 21.

Chapter 16
Wall Hanging with Ring

They are eye-catchers par excellence and shouldn't be missing in your home. Wall hangings can be made with metal rings or wood in wonderful ways. For this purpose, I'm presenting to you an easy-to-copy variant.

Material

- Ring
- Yarn
- Pair of scissors
- Pearls

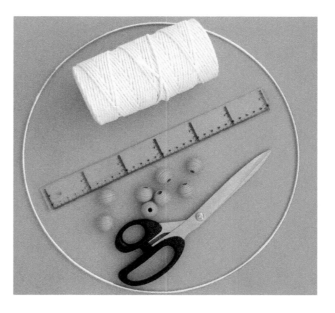

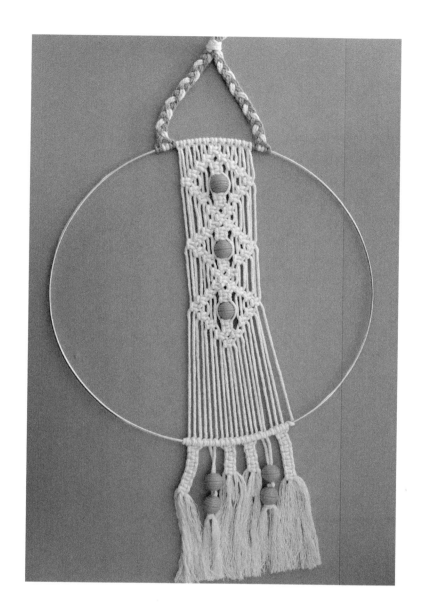

1

Cut to measure ten cords with a length of
120 cm, which you then fix to the ring
with an anchor knot. Then take another
cord, which is also fixed with an anchor
knot, and use it to divide the cords in the
middle. This cord is not supposed to be
very long. You will later use it as a hanger
or hook.

2

Try out yourself which way is the best op-
tion for you: Variant a) on the table or variant b) hooked to a cupboard or a door.

3

Put aside the eight outermost strands on
the left and right side. Now, you've got
four cords in the middle. These cords you
must use to make a carrick bend. Then put
aside the two strands on the right side.

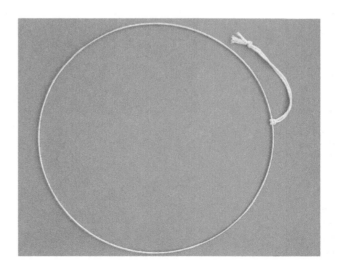

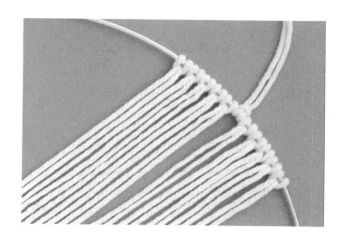

4

Now you've got two further strands in front of you which you need to proceed. Take two new strands of those you put aside to the left side. You've got four strands now, which you use to make into another carrick bend. Proceed like that until all of your strands on the left side have been tied to form a carrick bend. The result should be a row of down-running carrick bends. Repeat this procedure on the right side.

5

Now put the eight outermost strands aside again and make two carrick bends using the remaining strands. Then push a big pearl on the two middle strands and close up everything with two further carrick bends.

6

Proceed with a number of carrick bends which run straight from top to bottom.

7

Put aside the strands on the right side and start off working on the left side. The two outermost strands on the left side are put aside and proceed with the next four strands. After that, you put aside two further strands on the left side and, instead, add two strands on the right side. That's the way you proceed until you have tied all your strands into carrick bends.

8

Then repeat these steps on the right side. As a result, you should obtain what can be seen in the image. Repeat everything to get the same pattern again. Depending on the size of your ring, you may repeat the pattern three to four times,

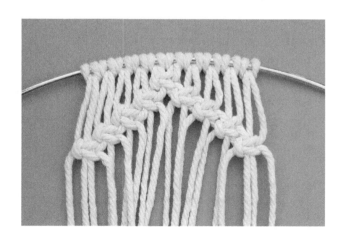

After you got to the bottom, the strands must be fixed to the ring to make sure the pattern won't shift. Wrap the cord around the ring once and pull it tight. Repeat this step and pass the cord through the loop.

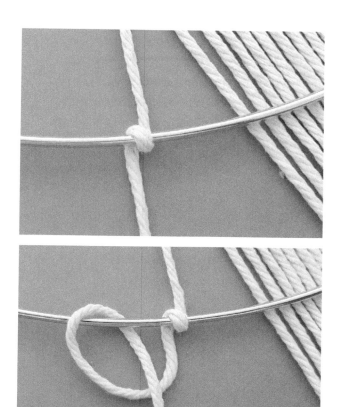

10

Then create further patterns with the remaining strands as you like. Or you can
comb them and cut them to measure. I decided to go for a mix of both variants.

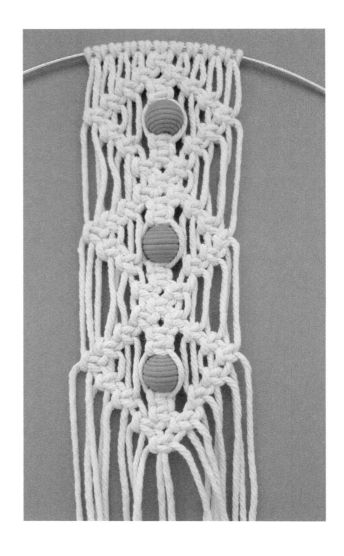

Chapter 17
Wall Hanging with Wood

There are many wonderful wall hangings that can be created with wood. In the following, you find an easy-to-copy example.

Materials

- Wood
- Macrame yarn
- Pair of scissors
- Wooden pearls
- 2 hooks

Step-by-Step Instructions

1

Cut to measure six cords with a length of about 120 cm, which you fix to a piece of wood. The knot you need is an anchor knot.

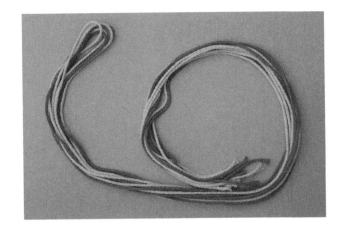

2

Now you can fix the hooks to a door or cupboard and feed your piece of wood into it.

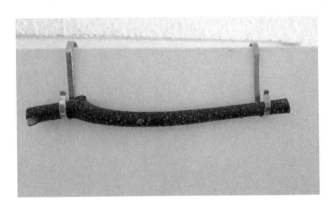

3

Then take the four strands on the left side and tie them into a carrick bend. You may hang up the remaining knots on the hook, so you won't get confused. Then put the four cords on the left side on the hook and take four more cords. You proceed like that until you've got a row of three carrick knots.

4

Then put two strands on the outer left side of the hook and continue working with the next four strands. Repeat everything with the next four strands. The result you should obtain are two carrick bends next to each other.

5

Place three cords on the hooks on the left and right side and continue working with the four middle strands. Now, you should have a triangle consisting of a total of six carrick bends, which are then surrounded by means of a clove hitch.

6

To achieve that, put the six cords on the right side of the hook and continue working on the left side only. Take the outermost cord on the left side and place it L-shaped over the other cords. Then take the cord next to it and wrap it around your L-shaped cord. Repeat everything twice.

7

Having proceeded in such a manner with all cords on the left side, continue with the right side. After that, you can tie your two working cords together twice.

8

Divide your 12 cords into three groups. Then take four cords and tie them into a row of wave knots. You tie a wave knot by means of a carrick bend, only that you start tying on the right side (or on the left side). This knot is also called half carrick bend.

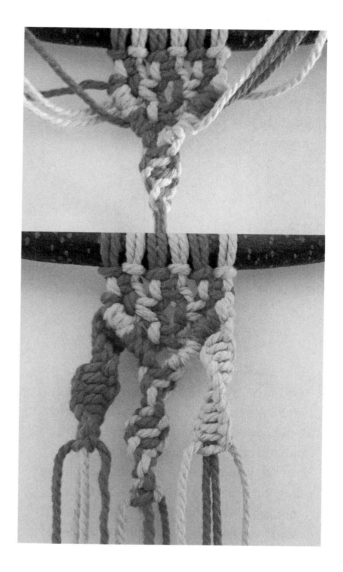

9

Repeat everything about ten times. Then push a wooden pearl on the two middle cords before you proceed with the wave knot.

10

Add two further cords on each side. You may take them to tie a long row of carrick bends or to choose a wave knot. If both outer strands have the right length, you can tie them to the other cords. To achieve that, put aside the outer cords on the left and right side, while the other cords remain in the middle. Then you make two or more carrick bends on top of them.

11

Having finished this step, you take your wall hanging off the hook and comb the ends nicely. After that, you cut them to measure.

12

In order to hang up your wall hanging, you may weave a cord and fix it to both ends of the wood.

Chapter 18
Macrame Heart

Which better way there is to say that you really like somebody than with a heart? You wish to give your mother a nice gift for Mother's Day? Perhaps you just wish to create a beautiful piece of decoration for your house? If yes, you're in the right place. I'm explaining to you how you can make yourself a Macrame heart.

Materials

- Macrame yarn
- Pair of scissors
- Comb
- Clipboard
- Dress-hanger
- Ruler

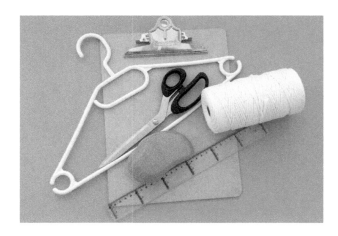

1

First, cut to measure twelve cords with a length of 70 cm and eight cords with a length of 20 cm. Then clamp the dress-hanger to the clipboard and tie the long cords fast to it by means of an anchor knot.

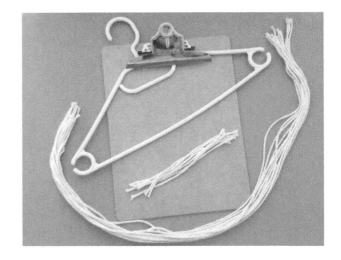

2

Put aside two cords on the left and right side. These are added later. Now you still have 20 cords in front of you. Take eight cords on each side and push them a bit aside. You have now four cords in the middle, which are also added only later. You may place them somewhere above the dress-hanger.

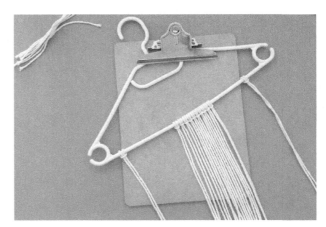

3

Then tie the first four knots on the left side into a carrick bend. To achieve that, take four cords. Place the left cord over the other cords and the right cord over it, then pass it behind the others and feed it into the L-loop. Pull the knot tight and repeat everything back-to-front.

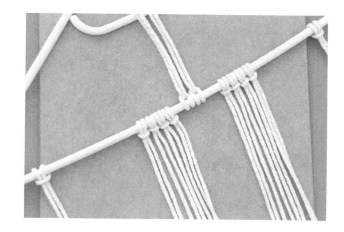

4

You proceed like that with the next four cords in the row, and on the right side. You have a row consisting of four carrick bends in front of you now. Now add the four upper cords as well as the other cords you put aside on each side.

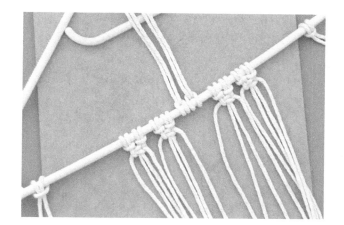

5

Take four cords and tie them into another row of carrick bends.

6

Put aside two cords on each side and take the remaining cords to tie them into a row of carrick bends. Then take one cord from each side and add it to the middle.

7

Tie two of the short cords to every separate cord and make an anchor knot. Ignore these cords for the time being.

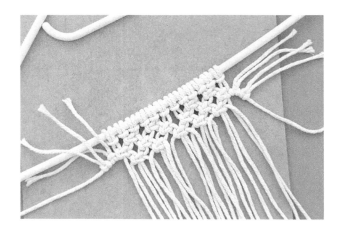

8

Take the long cords and tie them into another row of carrick bends. Then put aside two cords on each side before you make another row of carrick bends.

9

Tie two shorter cords to the outermost cords on the left and right side. Then create another row of carrick bends with all your cords.

10

Put aside two cords from each row on the left and right side, so you can create the tip of the heart.

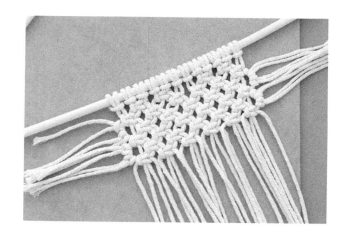

11

You've almost finished your piece of art. Now, take your pair of scissors and cut off the cords from the dress-hanger. Also, cut everything off round the heart. Comb the fringes out very carefully and, in case, trim them into form. And here we go! Your heart's finished.

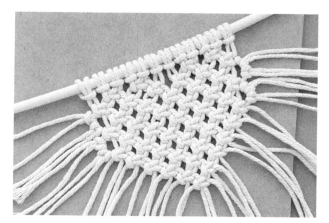

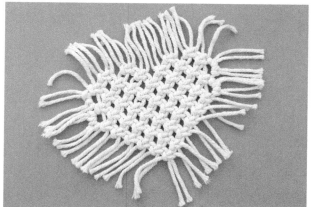

Chapter 19
Hanging Basket

Sometimes you've got the feeling you must decorate your home with wonderful plants and flowers. However, you don't want to place them on furniture for fear you could splash water on them when watering your plants. The windowsills are too small and your dreams of a beautiful green home are coming to naught. Or aren't they? Well, there is a way to fulfill your dreams, and that is with a Macrame hanging basket in which you can put your flowers and plants you wish to have at home. How you can easily create your own wonderful hanging basket, I'm explaining to you in the following instructions.

Materials

- 8 cords with a length of 4 m
- 2 cords with a length of 2 m
- Wooden ring
- Pair of scissors
- Pearls, if you like

1

Pass the eight long cords up to the middle of your wooden ring. The result is that you've got 16 cords with a length of 2 m each.

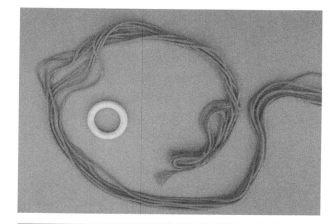

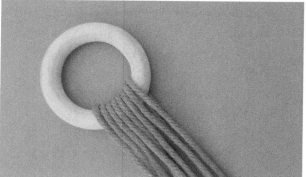

2

Place all 16 cords to form one thick bundle. Then place one of the shorter cords on top of it to produce a loop to the bottom. Wrap the cord several times around the bundle. Bring the end of the cord through the loop, take the upper end of the cord and pull the knot under the wrap. Your winding knot is completed now, and the longer cords are tightly fixed to the ring.

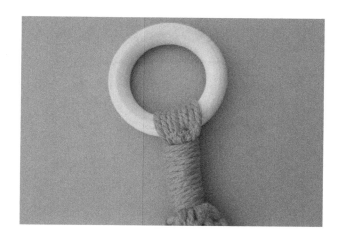

3

Take four of the cords next to each other and continue working. Put the other ones aside, you need them later. If you prefer working on the table, you can either fix the ring with regular scotch tape to your work pad, or you use a clipboard to make sure nothing can shift.

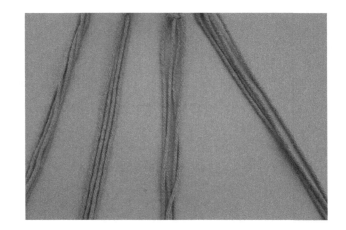

4

Then you tie the four cords into 15 carrick bends. Place four cords next to each other. Take the outermost cord on the left and place it L-shaped over the other cords. Then move the outer cord on the right over the L-shaped cord, under the middle cords and through the loop. Repeat everything back-to-front.

5

Having made the 15 carrick bends, the two middle cords are swapped with the outer cords. Why? This way we can make sure that the working cords retain a sufficient length. Carrick bends would reduce the length of the outer cords, while the middle cords won't be affected.

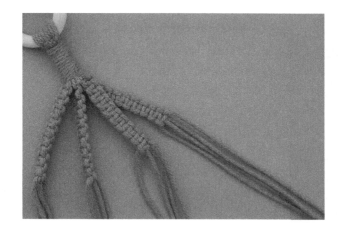

6

Now proceed with the half knot, also
called wave knot. It's basically the same
procedure as in the case of carrick bends.
The difference, however, is that you tie
from one side only. So, you've got the
choice to proceed with the left or right
side. After the third half knot, you will see
why this knot is also called wave knot.
Since we only tie the knot from one side,
our cord starts to spin. Best you make 20
half knots. But you may also extend your
row of carrick bends and leave the wave
knot out instead, as I did it. Both variants
look beautiful.

7

If you have finished knotting your wave,
you proceed with six new carrick bends.

8

Repeat these steps with all other cords,
and in the end, you will have four strands
consisting of carrick bends or half wave
knots.

9

Having finished all four strands, proceed as follows: Take two cords of one strand and add two more cords from the strand next to it. Measure about 20 cm off the pattern and create two carrick bends. Proceed like that with the remaining cords. Make sure that the distance to the first pattern always remains the same. Otherwise, your hanging basket will be sloping.

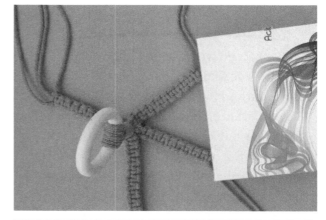

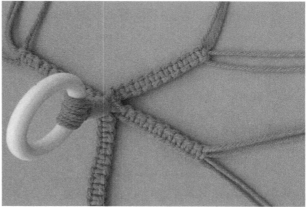

10

Having finished the work with all your cords, take two of a strand and combine them with two cords of the strand next to it. The distance to the last two carrick bends has been reduced to only 10 cm. Then make two more carrick bends.

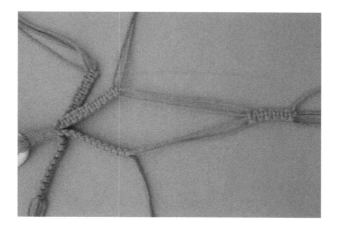

11

Having finished all strands, you tie together all cords under the carrick bends.
Then take the second cord with a length of
1 m, make it into a loop, wrap it around all
other cords, move its end through the
loop and pull the bend under the wrap
again.

12

You've almost finished your hanging lantern. What remains to be done is trim the
cords to the desired length.

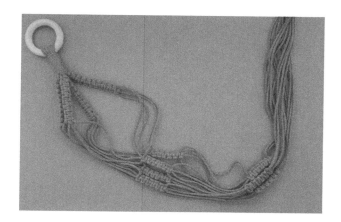

Advice:

If you wish to create an even more beautiful design, you may add a few pearls between the carrick bends.

The special feature of this hanging basket is that you can insert pots of various sizes or even jars. So what are you waiting for? Try it out yourself. I wish you all success and a lot of fun!

Chapter 20
Table Runner

Not only coasters, which I explained to you above, are real eye-catchers, but also Macrame table runners do the job. There are numerous variants you can make. I'm presenting to you one of the simple variants, which is easy-to-copy.

Materials

- Yarn
- Pair of scissors
- Bar or dress hanger

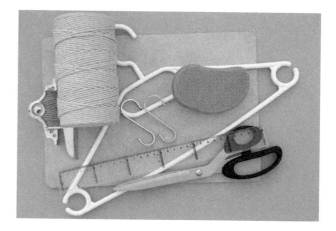

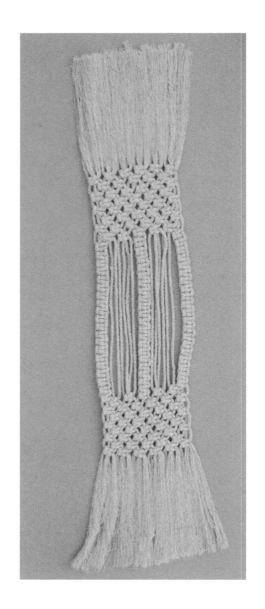

1

First, cut to measure twelve cords with a length of about 4 m which you fix to a dress-hanger by means of an anchor knot. You can clamp it to a clipboard or hang up on a door or cupboard door. That makes your work a lot easier.

2

Since your cords are very long, I recommend rolling them in and pull them tight with a simple yarn. Otherwise, they may get entangled, and it will take you a lot of additional work to disentangle them again.

3

Working with the door, you can cut to measure a piece of cardboard with a width of 10 cm and a length of 20 cm. Take some with duct tape and fix to the door in order to make sure there is a distance of 10 cm between the dress-hanger and the first row of carrick bends. This distance is needed to be able to fray the ends of the table runner.

4

Take the first four cords and tie them into a carrick bend, as you did before. Repeat this step for the entire row.

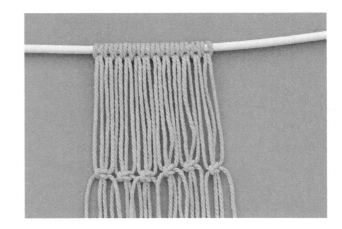

5

The second row will also be consisting of carrick bends. However, we choose the so-called offset carrick bend this time. To tie it, you put aside two cords on each side. You can either fix them by means of a duct tape or hang into the ends of the dress-hanger. Then take the next four cords and start off with the second row of carrick bends.

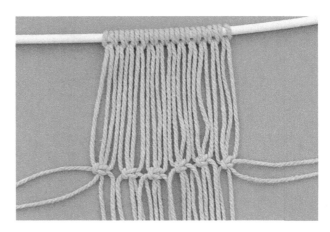

6

For the third row, you take the four cords you put aside in the second row. Repeat step 4) and make a third row of carrick bends.

7

You can continue this pattern as often as you like. I decided to make eight rows of bends.

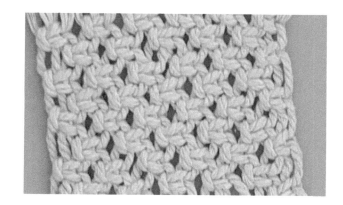

8

Having finished it, you can think about how to continue: You may create the whole table runner this way, or you may change the pattern every once in a while, like I did. I decided to tie a row of carrick bends to the bottom, leave out six cords, tie another row of 20 carrick bends, again leave out six cords, and finally tie a third row of carrick bends to the bottom.

9

After that, I tied eight rows of offset carrick bends again.

Before you tie your cords to the end, don't forget to measure, if there are about 10 cm left for fringes in order to give your table runner a uniform appearance. Then take your table runner from the dress-hanger by cutting the anchor knot open. Then carefully comb the ends of both sides, so your table runner can have beautiful fringes.

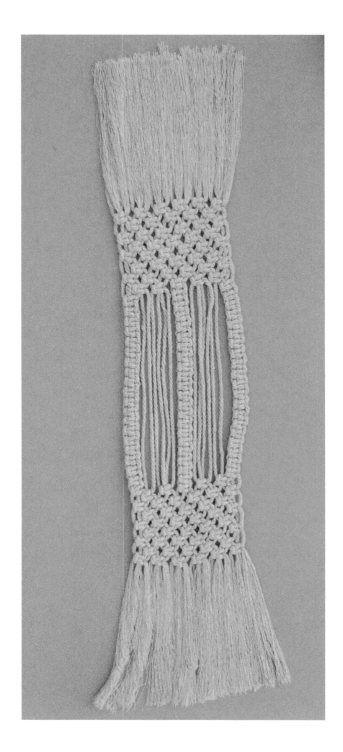

Advice:

If you wish to vamp up your table runner a bit, you may add some pearls to the mid-section of the triangles between the carrick bends. But don't forget that it will make it more difficult to place something on the table runner later.

Chapter 21
Dream-Catcher

This is an old Indian tradition, which is a matter of fascination for many other people, too. The dream-catcher, a mesh of threads fixed to a ring, embellished with pearls and feathers, is, when placed in the right place above the bed, meant to ward off bad dreams and instead catch good dreams.

Did you know that you make a dream-catcher by tying threads together? The Macrame knotting technique serves to create dream-catchers. The projects you got to know so far were quite easy and suitable for beginners. If tying threads has been fun for you up to now, and you're feeling ready to start off with something more complicated, the following instructions for creating a wonderful dream-catcher in form of a moon with many small pearls is just the right challenge for you. Take your time when reading through the various working steps, have a closer look at the images, and you will soon have made a beautiful dream-catcher yourself.

Materials

- Macrame yarn, white
- Pair of scissors
- Black pearls
- White, silver pearls
- Feathers
- Turquoise-coloured stones with holes
- Wooden pearls
- End caps
- Thin yarn
- Ring

1

First of all, you need to have a lot of patience because the entire ring must be covered by wraps of yarn. Best you take hot glue and fix the part you want to start off with to the ring, so nothing can shift while you work. When having reached your starting point again, you can cut the cord off the roll. Make sure it's long enough to form the loop for hanging up.

2

It's getting complicated now – but don't worry, it looks more complicated than it really is. You need the thin yarn and the turquoise-coloured stones, as well as a pin. Cut off a very long piece of yarn and tie one end of it tightly to the ring. The spot you choose for that should be about 10 cm apart from your hanging loop.

3

Then bring the first stone on the cord and push it up to the ring. After that you stick the pin under, then over the ring and finally pass it through the loop. Then pull the cord as tight as possible so that your stone is set firmly and won't shift. Proceed like that until your first row of stones is finished. Since it's a crescent, you should make sure not to close opening a) and prevent opening b) from becoming neither too big nor too small.

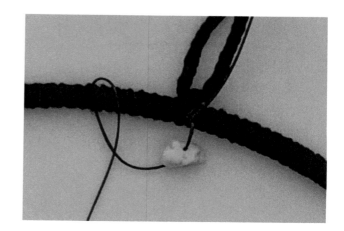

4

Your cord will have become very short now. Tie its end to the ring and cut to measure a new cord. What follows now is a row of white pearls. However, this row is not pulled tightly to the ring, but in the gaps between the stones. Then you proceed with a row of black pearls, which you handle in the same manner.

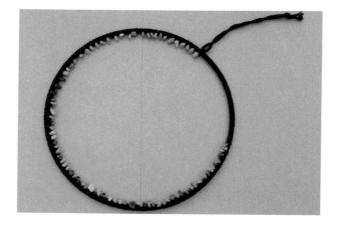

5

Now, it's time for a mesh of threads proceed as before, only without using pearls and small stones. Always hold the knot with the thumb and index finger of your left hand to prevent the mesh from becoming too loose.

6

In order to finalize the crescent in a beautiful way, you may fix another row of white, silver or black pearls.

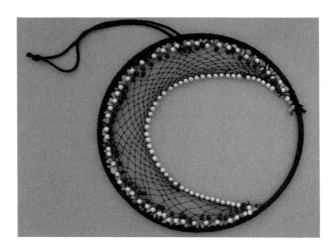

7

Your dream-catcher is almost finished. Only feathers are missing. Fix threads to the bottom part of your ring on which you can push pearls. Or you leave it the way it is and only fix feathers to the bottom part. I decided to create a mix of both variants. So, I pushed blue wooden pearls on the longer threads, to which they were fixed by means of a bit of hot glue. Then I glued the feathers to the bottom pearls.

8

But you can also proceed as I did with the shorter threads. Glue end caps to the threads. Then take your thin yarn and bring the feathers through the opening of the end caps. Now your dream-catcher is finished!

Advice:

If you wish to have more decoration, you may add further elements to your dream-catcher. There's no limit to what you may create.

Chapter 22
Angels

Particularly when Christmas time has come, you may often wonder which gift you could give to your beloved ones. Often, it's hard to find something "unique". What about a Macrame angel this year? All you need for making one, is Macrame yarn, pearls and a wooden ring. Well, I forgot, of course you need some patience and enthusiasm to create it.

Materials

- Macrame yarn, white
- Pair of scissors
- Wooden ball
- Wooden ring
- Comb
- Thin yarn

1

You need 12 cords with a length of 35 cm. Also, cut to measure 6 further cords with a length of 30 cm. Another cord with a length of 50 cm will also be necessary to be used to fix your ball.

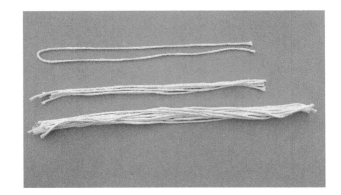

2

Double the cord with a length of 50 cm. Push it with the loop through the wooden ring. Then pull the loose ends through it in order to tighten the cord to the ring.

3

Then bring the ball on both loose ends. You may use a crotchet hook for this purpose, which facilitates this step. Push the ball up to the upper rim of the ring, while the cords should be under the ring.

4

Then place the right cord over the ring, thus producing a loop. Move it through the loop and tighten it. Repeat everything, so the cord can have proper support. Proceed like that with the left cord. Now, your ball can't shift anymore.

5

Now the six other cords with a length of 30 cm will be combed. Take three of them and apply your comb. Bring the bundle through the ring to be on the left side of the ball. Repeat this step with the remaining three cords and bring these through the ring to be on the right side of the ball.

6

With a thin yarn in a colour of your choice, you can wrap a winding knot around the two bundles now. This is your angel's beautiful belt. Double the working cord. Tie the bottom end as often as possible around the filler cords. Then pass the winding knot through the loop and pull its upper end up in order to cause the knot to disappear under the wrap. Cut off both ends of the wrap.

7

In order to hang up your angel later, make an anchor knot (see step 1) and use it to fix a cord with a length of 20 cm above the ball.

8

Use an anchor knot to fix one half of the cords with a length of 35 cm to the left side of the ring and the other half of the cords to the right side of the ring.

9

Take your yarn roll and roll off a good piece of yarn without cutting it off. Then place this cord to the cords on the left side. This is your working knot, to which you tie a row of reef knots. Start off with the first cord on top and tie it around the cord placed next to it as follows: Place the loop cord L-shaped over your working cord. Take the loose end of the loop cord and pass it under the working cord, over it and then through the loop. Repeat everything or the cord won't be fitting properly. It's important to tighten the loop cords only. Repeat the looping with all cords on the left side.

10

When having looped the last cords on the left side, you can cut the working cord off the yarn so that it will have the same length as the other cords. Repeat the looping on the right side.

Advice:
Use a pin board to make sure nothing can shift.

Important:
The reef knot must always be pulled tight in order to avoid creating gaps.

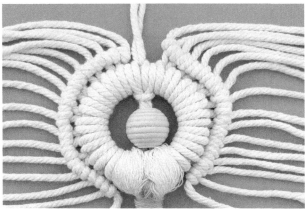

11

Comb your cords well and trim the wings of the angel to measure.

12

In order to stabilize the wings, you may apply hairspray.

Chapter 23
The Perfect Macrame Work-Place

You have been informed about so many Macrame projects – but how the perfect Macrame work-place does look like, you don't really know yet. That's why I'd like to give you a short summary on it.

For more complex Macrame projects, I recommend you use a rolling garment rail. It's not expensive and easy to stow away and get out again. If you wish to knot fewer complex projects, you can work on your table or quite comfortably on your sofa. Just use a clipboard or a cork plate.

In order to facilitate the decision pro or contra a garment rail for you, I'd like to let you know briefly for which Macrame projects it's suitable in many wonderful ways:

- Wall hangings
- Hanging baskets
- Table runners
- Blankets
- Bags
- Scarves

Should you wonder how you could fix the material to the rail without cutting it open, I can make the following suggestions and let you know a few tips and tricks:

Just take small hooks for hanging up or fix your project by means of cable straps.

On a cork plate or a clipboard, you may put the following Macrame projects into practice:

- Garlands
- Feathers
- Hearts
- Key chains
- Jewellery
- Rainbows
- Wristbands
- Friendship bands and many things more

A cork plate is particularly suited for all these projects, since you can easily fix things with pins on them.

23.1 How to stow away materials in a practical way

People who once got into Macrame won't probably get away from it so soon again. That also means that you need to keep a certain quantity of material in your home stocks. The question arises how you can or should store all those things you need.

The best method is you get yourself a number of baskets that you can stow away on shelves or closable boxes. So, you can easily store your yarns and other materials in them. Remaining yarns or pins as well as other small parts can best be stored in closable cans. If you additionally label them, you don't even have to search long for what you need for your Macrame projects.

Closing Remarks

In the last years, Macrame has become a popular trend if it comes to manufacturing home decorations, table decorations and other nice components of people's style of living. Since there are many different Macrame techniques, every knotting project which you finish will become a real attraction in the eyes of all those people you present it as a gift. You will make them happy, and they will be full of fascination for it – since every knotting project is unique.

Once you found your way into the world of many knots, you will soon realize that some knotting projects look much more complicated than their making really is.

If you wish to rehearse making the knots without starting off with a Macrame project as such, just take the threads you need and try to tie the different knots again and again until you've got the proper expertise.

Macrame is a wonderful hobby that makes time to fly. It also helps you to forget all sorrows in a truly magical manner, since you have to focus completely on your knotting project.

Once you've started with Macrame and have mastered the basic techniques, you will accept new challenges and try out more complicated projects to keep surprising your beloved ones with new gifts.

By the way, if you know your way around Macrame techniques, you will someday be able to design completely new patterns and layout new projects.

I hope that by reading this book your interest in the art of Macrame could be kindled and that you're feeling that Macrame fervour within you now. All instructions you find in this book have been carefully selected to make it easier for beginners to quickly familiarize with Macrame.

I wish you a good supply of yarn for all your future projects, and have a lot of fun in creating unique pieces of art.

Did you enjoy this book?

Dear Readers,

Are you happy with this book? Is it meeting your expectations?

I would be pleased to receive your feedback on Amazon and give me the chance to improve.

Thank you in advance!

Cordially yours,

Vivien Romhoffer

Disclaimer

The implementation of all information, instructions and strategies contained in this book is at your own risk. The author cannot be held liable for any damages of any kind for any legal reason. Liability claims against the author for material or non-material damages caused by the use or non-use of the information or by the use of incorrect and/or incomplete information are excluded in principle. Therefore, any legal and damage claims are also excluded. This work was compiled and written down with the greatest care and to the best of our knowledge. However, the author accepts no responsibility for the topicality, completeness and quality of the information. Printing errors and misinformation cannot be completely excluded. No legal responsibility or liability of any kind can be assumed for incorrect information provided by the author.

Copyright

All contents of this work as well as information, strategies and tips are protected by copyright. All rights are reserved. Any reprint or reproduction - even in part - in any form such as photocopying or similar processes, saving, processing, copying and distribution by means of electronic systems of any kind (in whole or in part) is strictly prohibited without the express written permission of the author. All translation rights reserved. The contents may not be published under any circumstances. The author reserves the right to take legal action in case of disregard.

Impressum

© Vivien Romhoffer
2023
1st edition
All rights reserved.
Reprinting, even in extracts, is not permitted.
No part of this work may be reproduced, duplicated or distributed in any form without the written permission of the author.
Contact us: Mark Lipke, Kuhanger 9, 31787 Hameln-Germany
Cover design: B.M.
Cover:Deposit

Printed in Great Britain
by Amazon